My Brother Ate My Homework

Kyla Walker

PAGE PUBLISHING, INC.
Conneaut Lake, PA

First originally published by Page Publishing 2021

ISBN 978-1-6624-2460-1 (pbk)
ISBN 978-1-6624-2461-8 (digital)

Printed in the United States of America

Although no Walk
Although no Talk
You've taught us to Love,
Have Faith & Have Hope.

—Forever Kaisah, October 7, 2017

No one believes that my brother ate my homework.

I love my baby brother,

but I noticed he likes to get me in trouble a lot.

He even empties out my shoe rack. My parents are always yelling "Kyla, why are your sneakers all over the place!"

One time, I had a really
important assignment.

It was very hard, but of course, I got it done. I was super proud of myself.

"Kyla, did you finish your homework!"
Mommy yells out.

"Yes, Mommy, it's right here on the table. Let me show you."

"But...but it was just right here!"

"KAZEEEEEEEEEEEE!"

9

Why would you do this, baby brother?

Since my baby brother ate my homework, I had to complete the assignment all over again.

Although he can be
my nemesis, he is
still my little brother.

13

The End

14

About the Author

Kyla Walker is a seven-year-old girl from the Bronx, New York. The book *My Brother Ate My Homework* is the first to her trilogy. She was the youngest of two until two years ago. She now reveals what it is like living with her baby brother.

CPSIA information can be obtained
at www.ICGtesting.com
Printed in the USA
BVHW060515030921
615367BV00002B/2